Quotes That Keep You Afloat

by

Bobby and Seini Acres

RoseDog Books
PITTSBURGH, PENNSYLVANIA 15238

RoseDog Books
585 Alpha Drive
Suite 103
Pittsburgh, PA 15238
Visit our website at *www.rosedogbookstore.com*

ISBN: 978-1-6461-0362-1
eISBN: 978-1-6461-0408-6

Sometimes all it takes is a word of encouragement to make a person day. A positive quote can stick with you throughout your journey in life; we've heard people repeat old quotes they heard from their grandparents by saying" my grandmother use to say". A good quote can stick with you instantly especially when you can relate to the meaning. My wife Seini and I wanted to give you these jewels that you can use throughout life that can help you appreciate the sun and learn how to dance in the rain.

When no one could see I believed in me

Wearing the mask of laughter only shows you're a good actor

Right isn't right when it's the wrong person

Pretending it don't exist doesn't mean it don't exist

Getting blinded by emotions can limit your greatness

Good ADVICE RATHER GIVEN OR TAKEN HELPS you AWAKEN

When you keep looking in the rear view mirror
you're bound to miss what's in front of you.

When you do average things you get average results

In the word disable you will find able

Just because drama knocks on your door
there's no need to invite it in

It's difficult to bounce a ball of emotions

The only way to float above adversity is by taking a leap of faith

For every high there's a blessing for every low there's a lesson

When you live for others the real you is undiscovered

My better half made a better me

REALIZING YOUR WEAKNESS IS REALIZING YOUR STRENGTHS

Misery always needs a friend

When your life becomes a circus be the ringmaster

You can't see worth in a worthless mind

Learn to stay in orbit

While most settle continue to pedal through life

Make sure your train of thought is on schedule

When you define each other you complete the puzzle

THE SNAIL CAN'T TELL THE EAGLE HOW TO FLY

Even when you're outnumbered refuse to be conquered

Truth makes the writing on the wall legible

Failure is a mind state

You can't complain if you don't work toward change

When your foundation is cemented
nothing falls through the cracks

You're usually mislead if you react off what they said

Love has no ceilings when you unmask your feelings

BE BLESSED BY BLESSING OTHERS

Let your book of life be a best seller

YOUR CLOUD CAN'T STOP MY REIGN

A GROWN GIRL needs to grow into womanhood

YOU CAN'T SEE THE PICTURE WITH AN UNDEVELOPED MIND

You're never lost when you got direction

Pain is growth to succeed you need both

Whenever light insist darkness can't exist

Stay true and you can break through

ALTHOUGH LOVE IS FREE IT MAY COST YOU

THERE'S NO RETURN FOR KINDNESS

Love is finding life on her/his planet

When the devil's invited a house becomes divided

Gossip is like a leaky faucet every drip seems to drain

You can't feel sorry for sorry people

There's no audience for attention grabbers

If you don't grow together you'll grow apart

No one passes when the memory is everlasting

The very thing that glitters oftentimes slitters

Your reflection knows your imperfections

Escape the shadow by stepping into the light

A great leader still can follow directions

Your eyes can't judge the size of a person heart

If freedom has a cost what are you willing to pay

It's all forgotten but not forgiven

LIVE LIFE OUTSIDE THE MARGINS

THE SAME ONES YOU MISTREATED
YOU'LL REALIZE YOU NEEDED

The early bird gets the final word

In order to take the high road you must know the zip code

Life has crooks and turns but in the end you learn

When you look in the mirror know you can deliver

PRESSURE ELIMINATES THE Lesser

A true leader is a servant of the people

As your path guide you your purpose will find you

When you complacent you accept limitations

When the minds clouded it's hard to fly around it

Don't take kindness for blindness

A SHEEP CAN'T STEP IN THE LIONS DEN

You can't drive forward when your life is in reverse

Stress is given as a test it's up to you to pass or fail

A thinker thinks and a knower does

Govern your state of mind

NOWADAYS A real man is in high demand

Hurt feelings aren't always revealing

Giving your best is always the best way forward

THE ONLY WAY TO BE THE NEXT MAN UP
IS TO OUTWORK THE NEXT MAN

A know it all is the first to fall

Love is taking pleasure in growing old together

See the real you by stepping out your comfort zone

When your soul rejoice that means you can hear god's voice

When you plan to build you build your plan

Most limits are invented in your mind

To reach the top it starts with one building block

Those that complain will always remain

Take a stance to look beyond your circumstance

You can't stand to the side and say you tried

When you awake you'll rather give then take

Don't be a prop in your on movie

With one stroke God decorated the face of the Earth

My truth remains even after my remains

You're in the driver's seat with no drive

Don't rent me if you with me

The right advice can give you life

Because of my belief I reach

Superman don't send clark kent to the rescue

You can't crop the picture of life

Those that wait get weighted down
those that seek find higher ground

Just because you fell don't mean you failed

MARRIAGE IS BETWEEN TWO NOT THE WORLD
BUT TOGETHER YOU CAN CONQUER THE WORLD

Only with god you can defy all odds

Your net won't get you respect

THE GREATEST DESKIES IS WHEN YOU BELIEVE YOUR LIES

No one dreams to be a failure

What I gave you can save you

The only way to test your wings is to leave the nest

Because I love me you and I can AGREE

WHEN THE WORLD HURTS THE PLANET CRIES

YOU CAN HAVE IT ALL AND STILL HAVE NOTHING

If you don't make the call you won't receive answered prayers

When you raise the stakes sell the plates

One of us means all of us together we can't fail

Showing up isn't good enough

You can waste time but don't waste mine

The person that corrects you respects you

You can look the part and not play the role

Put fear to the rear and let it push you forward

When you thought I was done I already won

Knowing your self-worth eliminates self-doubt

Stop yapping and show action

EMPOWER YOURSELF BY EMPOWERING OTHERS

Change for the better makes a better tomorrow

To share a life with one another is like no other

Even when it's hard times continue to climb

Go through it get through it

Sometimes you have to regroup and reboot

Give your purpose time to surface

A no it all don't know enough

How can you run your life when you running your mouth

CHOOSE WHAT'S RIGHT BEFORE YOU CHOOSE TO FIGHT

No drive no prize

You're never done when you go beyond

There's no class for a school of sharks

You can peak at your lowest point

Just because you didn't pick the cards
don't mean you can't defy the odds

You can Fool everyone else but not yourself

The healing starts when you kneeling

The same ones that cheer you will smear you

MARRIAGE IS NOT AN OPEN BOOK FOR OTHERS TO READ

When you have business of your own you mind your on business

When things get heated keep a cool head

To pull through focus on you

Even when you quit your problem still exist

Don't compete if you accept defeat

You're not great if you just participate

Regardless of who delivers the message it's up to you to accept it

No need to lone for acceptance when you accept who you are

Plug into your inner self and take advantage of the outlets

Be in the moment

Your start is not where you make your mark

When everybody flee count on me

It's the tough times that define who you are

Let your purpose surface

Beauty is more then what the mirror reflects

Good advice can save your life

Don't let fear stir you in the wrong direction

Just because we're different don't mean we have to be indifferent

You become your own worst enemy
by wagging war against yourself

Don't confuse your pit stop as a final destination

Don't become a part of the finna family

The confused always finds a way to lose

Living in the free world don't mean you can freeload

You not wasting time when time is used wisely

Your mind is a universe it can either be a galaxy or a few stars

It's up to you to be at the door of opportunity

Stop focusing on being politically correct and just be correct

For you my life is a blog for me I defied the odds

Don't let a brand name make you act brand new

We in the microwave age where everything is ready made

Be the architect and build yourself

Even though we been typecast and cast away
somehow we found a way

A million ants can make a stance

A lot of imposters are found in the in crowd

Anger is too heavy to hold

Sometimes you have to distance yourself
from those that won't help themselves

Check your closet before you have a bone to pick

What I learned in the valley helped me to climb the mountain

You get drained supplying a blood sucker

The alligator never asked to be shoes

Your true self is found by who you hang around

There's no shelf life for doing what's right

A hot head will never get ahead

Basic doesn't equal greatness

There are no friends in a room full of yes men

Choosing not to be afraid is choosing to be free

No defense can block my goals

When you prepare the feast you deserve to eat

Success has a price tag

People that doubt your drive chose to abandon their ride

It's your responsible to carry your own baggage

Being unique is being complete

If you could see into your future you would never take chances

The music never stops for those that dance around there problems

Success cost but it don't have to be at the expense of others

Love the body you have because it's the only body you have

When you listen to everyone else opinion
it's hard to form your own

Exercise your thoughts to build your mind

One bad chapter in your life doesn't define your book

She went from anyone to my only one

DON'T CONFUSE YOUR CURRENT SITUATION FOR A PER-
MANENT SITUATION

You believed in me when I couldn't see

In order to free your mind you first have to unlock it

FINDING MEANING IN THE THINGS YOU LOVE
IS FINDING A PIECE OF YOURSELF

As your circle gets smaller your view gets wider

It's more than meets the eye when the eye sees more

A sprinkle of faith a dash of hope mixed with
a teaspoon of effort is the recipe for success

Just because I don't say don't mean I don't see

When you live on the edge sometimes you forget the ledge

Inspiration comes from the inner soul

Excuses and bad habits are hard to break

NEGATIVITY IS LIKE A VIRUS DON'T LET IT AFFECT YOU

You can be comfortable and miserable at the same time

People ignore until it knocks on their door

If they not improving keep it moving

Getting lost in love helped me find myself

When confusion flares up get a dose of understanding

Turn down the noise in your head

The planet is your home court

Just because your parents give you everything
doesn't mean the world will

Master the art of getting up

Recover from a misstep by making your next step the right step

Action picks up where words left off

Don't bend over backwards for those
that try to get you bent out of shape

True love don't mind being locked in the chambers of his/her heart

It's easy to blame the puppet

You'll never heal by wishing others ill will

Don't let what's at stake get peppered

When god say jump it's not because you can fly
it's because he'll catch you

Sometimes you got to get lost in order to find yourself

When you at the top images at the bottom appear smaller

You can improve talent but you can't donate heart

Who needs a compass when you on the road to accomplish

It's going to take all of us to save one of us

Don't get so distracted by race that you forget you're in a race

A beautiful illusion is still a trick

Start living your vision

You have to leave those that don't believe

Don't get trapped in what was that you can't see what is

A closed mind only sees the world through a peep hole

Just because you planted a seed today
don't mean it'll bare fruit tomorrow

Don't down yourself crown yourself

Everything good that comes through me comes from he

The king and the jester doesn't share the same problems

Choose to float while others parade around

When you face the bully you erase the bully

What's in stock isn't necessarily what's in store

Yesterday won't pay for today

Wisdom speaks in places the youth can't interpret

Your thinking cap ain't the only one that fits

You can't only be strong when the lights on

What's at your core defines you more

Either step forward or step aside

Look forward even when you get looked over

On the highway of life put on your hazards

Everybody is the man until the man shows up

AFTER YOU PRAY GO MAKE A WAY

When you gave all that you got to give
it takes a little more to get up the hill

BIG DREAMS DON'T SPEAK TO SMALL EFFORT

Pull your weight don't pull me down

You either lead or get led fish or get fed

You want the life but you don't want the strife

It's not what you don't know it's what you refuse to learn

If you scared of the unseen you'll never grow wings

SILENCE IS A SOUND THAT HAS DIED

I exemplify results while you exemplify excuses

All success has a risk factor

You can't steer around fear

Sometimes things are the way they are for a reason

Learn to laugh learn to live

When the woman's damaged the planet becomes unbalanced

Don't wanna hear about your glory days what you doing nowadays

Being down is a part of life don't make staying down a part of you

You love social media but lack social skills

IF you can't feel you can't heal

Just because our stories differ don't mean mine don't exist

The fool is the last to know

KARMA SHOWS NO FAVORITES

Because you don't have what it takes
don't hate on the ones that do

YOU CAN'T THINK DIFFERENT AND DO THE SAME

Enjoy life you only get a one way trip

When you think you can't go no more the more you can go

Trust shouldn't feel like cuffs

A BETTER ME MAKES A BETTER WE

You was the flame that fueled me

Clean up your act by dusting off old habits

You're not a lost cause you lost cause you gave up

Pull through by being the best you

Don't be jealous of what I've become if you haven't did what I done

I BE ABOUT IT WHILE YOU BLOG ABOUT IT

Sons carry the name daughters carry the life

Make it happen before it happens to you

Not understanding the plight means he only grew in height

When you pay the cost keep the receipts

Confidence gets you off the fence

To raise the bar keep your chin up

Committing to health is a Commitment to self

MONEY DON'T GROW ON TREES BUT EXCUSES DO

Don't confuse nonsense sense for common sense

WHEN you feel under pressure
put the pressure under you and rise to the occasion

When you come out the shell you unveil the real you

When god stamped you tailor made
don't worry about being the perfect fit

Your womb can open the door for a better tomorrow

When you hate yourself you hate everyone else

You take everything except advice

How you perform in a storm defines who you are

You can reach the sky if you willing to try

In order to get to the other side of the road
you got to go through traffic